Keep Life
Simple

T H E R A P Y

D1809538

Keep Life Simple
THERAPY

Written by
Linus Mundy

Illustrated by
R. W. Alley

GODSFIELD
PRESS

Copyright © 1995 *Godsfield Press Ltd*

Text © 1995 *Linus Mundy*

Illustrations © 1995 *R. W. Alley*

Originally published in the US by Abbey Press 1987

Published in the UK by Godsfield Press Ltd 1995

Cover Design by *The Bridgewater Book Company Ltd*

ISBN 1 899434 40 2

Write to

GODSFIELD PRESS LTD

Bowland House

off West Street, Alresford

Hants SO24 9AT

The right of *Linus Mundy* and *R. W. Alley* to be identified as
author and illustrator of this work has been asserted by them in
accordance with the Copyright, Designs and
Patents Act 1988

A CIP catalogue record for this book is available
from the British Library

Printed and bound in the UK

Foreword

Life is a complicated affair. Too much to do; too little time. Too many demands; too few resources. Too much commotion and busy-ness; too little peace and quiet.

The answer? *An* answer: Choosing to reduce life to its essence and keep it simple (or, at least, simpler). The fruits of this choice (and really it is hundreds of *little* choices rather than one big one) are substantial:

- By living more simply, we free up our overtaxed personal resources—our minds, our emotions, our spirits—from anxiety.
- By living more simply, we free up some of our world's relentlessly overtaxed natural resources.
- By living more simply, we shorten our list of "stuff" to care about, which gives us the chance to care *more* about what (and whom) is left.
- By living more simply, we open up our hearts to receive and be one with our "Supernatural Resource," our God who loves us and wants—very simply—only our good.

If you yearn to experience how less can be more, let *Keep-life-simple Therapy* be your gentle guide to what is truly essential.

1.

Reduce life to its essence. It is mostly love that matters...and lasts.

2.

Reduce love to its essence. It is mostly a knowing and a being known. Make the effort, do the work, of getting to know and letting your true self be known. You will see the oneness of love and Love.

3.

Learn the art of saying "no."
When you <u>exc</u>lude something,
you invariably <u>in</u>clude
something else even more
fully.

4.

Welcome your role in the drama of creation. Imagine the part you play as a leading role (which it is). But once in a while, keep still and let God speak the parts.

5.

Celebrate the ordinary. Your heart knows the comfort and the beauty in common things. Let it tell your head.

6.

Don't expect so much from <u>more</u>—and so little from <u>less</u>. Expect a <u>lot</u> from <u>less</u>. You won't be disappointed.

7.

It is hard to know when you "have enough." Make the question "Do I really need more?" part of your life's work.

8.

Look to nature for nurture. It is as reliable as the God who provides it.

9.

When making choices, opt for the plain, the simple, the functional. Less goes wrong when you stick to life's standard equipment.

10.

Do not pretend to be anything you are not. That way you can always be consistent and truly free.

11.

Live in time. Rushing to get one thing over so you can move on to something "more important" is folly.

12.

Practice being content. It is both the work and the reward of a lifetime.

13.

There is a time for doing—and a time for doing nothing. Don't underestimate the value of porch-sitting and rocking-chairing. They are simple gifts you can give to yourself—and others.

14.

Live intentionally. Forget that and your life will be lived for you.

15.

Learn to value spiritual things over material things. They last longer, cost less, bring more.

16.

Let manual labor, hard work, be a part of your life. You'll be proud of how humble it makes you.

17.

Be small and child-like. There is no simpler, better way to see the big picture.

18.

Try to eat and live lower on the food and resources chain. You'll be doing a world of good to beings yet unborn.

19.

Silence is golden. Seek it and it will quietly enrich your life.

20.

Get alone. It is one sure way of getting yourself together.

21.

Trust that God supplies you with unlimited good. There is grain left in the field even after the harvest.

22.

Remember that the primary reward of work is finding meaning and well-being, not money. Forget that and you'll stop being well.

23.

Set your desk, your chair, your sink, your sights with a view to the great outdoors. Life is simpler out there.

24.

Don't take your life too seriously. Trust in a God who cares for your every need.

25.

Don't let work and play be rivals. While each may have its separate place at times, both can also occupy the same space.

26.

Know your limits. There is nothing more freeing—or more motivating—than knowing what you can and cannot do well.

27.

Learn from life's oldest living things: trees. They impressively break forth with buds and colors—but know innately when it's time to shut down and be unimpressive.

28.

Strive to have access _to_ things, not ownership _of_ them. Possess something and it possesses you.

29.

Create a ten-second wildflower meadow in your mind whenever you need it. Your imagination can be a great peacemaker in times of chaos.

30.

Think small. Planting tiny seeds in the small space given to you can change the whole world—or, at the very least, your view of it.

31.

Cultivate the simple virtue of patience. Anticipation is not the only reward for waiting.

32.

Don't forget that the longing for simplicity is a spiritual longing. Asking physical things to meet spiritual needs doesn't work.

The
VERY
BIG
STORE

33.

Do only one thing at a time. Putting yourself wholeheartedly into what you are doing—no matter how small or mundane—honors it…and you…and your Creator.

34.

Rediscover the joy of a quiet conversation, a simple story or game, an honest expression of affection for another. These simple gifts and pleasures will help keep your life balanced.

35.

Know that your true home is in the holy Presence. It's that simple. Don't wait for your calendar to be empty, or your permanent address to change, before recognizing that reality.

ıus Mundy, publisher at Abbey Press, is the author of
ᵉ Elf-help Book *Slow-down Therapy*. He lives with his
.fe and three children in Santa Claus, Indiana.

.lustrator for the Abbey Press Elf-help Books, **R.W. Alley**
ılso illustrates and writes children's books. He lives in
Barrington, Rhode Island, with his wife and daughter.

**Elf-help Books . . . adding "a little character"
and a lot of help to self-help reading!**

Keep-life-simple Therapy
#20185-5 $3.95   ISBN 0-87029-257-9

Be-good-to-your-body Therapy
#20188-9 $3.95   ISBN 0-87029-255-2

Celebrate-your-womanhood Therapy
#20189-7 $3.95   ISBN 0-87029-254-4

Acceptance Therapy
#20190-5 $3.95   ISBN 0-87029-245-5

Keeping-up-your-spirits Therapy
#20195-4 $3.95   ISBN 0-87029-242-0

Play Therapy
#20200-2 $3.95   ISBN 0-87029-233-1

Slow-down Therapy
#20203-6 $3.95   ISBN 0-87029-229-3

Be-good-to-yourself Therapy
#20255-6 $3.95   ISBN 0-87029-209-9

Prayer Therapy
#20206-9 $3.95   ISBN 0-87029-225-0

Be-good-to-your-marriage Therapy
#20205-1 $3.95   ISBN 0-87029-224-2

One-day-at-a-time Therapy
#20204-4 $3.95   ISBN 0-87029-228-5

Available at your favorite bookstore or directly from us at:
Abbey Press Publications, St. Meinrad, IN 47577.
Phone orders: Call 1-800-325-2511.